IT WAS ALWAYS ME

IRA DANELLE PINKNEY

Scripture quotations marked (ESV) are taken from THE HOLY BIBLE,
ENGLISH STANDARD VERSION®, Copyright© 2001 by Crossway,
a publishing ministry of Good News Publishers. Used by permission.

Scripture quotations are taken from THE HOLY BIBLE, NEW
INTERNATIONAL VERSION®. Copyright© 1973, 1978, 1984,
2011 by Biblica, Inc.™. Used by permission of Zondervan.

Printed by Prize Publishing House, LLC in the United States of America.

First printing edition 2025.

Prize Publishing House
P.O. Box 9856, Chesapeake, VA 23321
www.PrizePublishingHouse.com

ISBN (Paperback): 979-8-9929954-2-8
ISBN (Hardcover): 979-8-9929954-3-5
ISBN (E-Book): 979-8-9929954-4-2

Library of Congress Control Number: 2026900129

CONTENTS

Dedication v

Foreword vii

Preface ix

Introduction xiii

CHAPTERS

1	What In The World Will I Do? 1
2	Facing The Reality of My Fears 17
3	The Silent Shame. 29
4	Look Who I Found 40
5	Starting From Scratch 57
6	It's Painful, But It's Necessary 71

DEDICATION

This book is dedicated to anyone who has experienced an identity crisis. May you never find yourself in that posture again.

To my children, thank you for loving me even on days when I was not at my best.

To my grandson Jaycen, MiMi loves you and promises to leave a legacy not only for you but also for your children's children.

And last but not least, I dedicate this book to myself. I am so proud of you, Ira, for not giving up on yourself. You did not allow the cares of this world to win.

FOREWORD

It is with considerable pride and heartfelt admiration that I introduce this powerful work, *It Was Always Me*, written by my dear cousin, Ira Danelle Pinkney. From the moment I began reading, I was captivated not only by the raw honesty of her words but also by the incredible bravery it took to share such a deep personal journey with the world.

In these pages, Ira lays her soul bare, and in doing so, has created something truly special. I found myself chuckling at her candid humor, pausing to reflect on her profound insights, and feeling a deep sense of connection as I saw my own experiences mirrored in her story. This book is a testament to the fact that while our paths may be unique, the struggles of the heart and the search for our true selves are universal.

It Was Always Me is more than just a memoir; it

is a guidebook for anyone who has ever felt lost, questioned their worth, or battled to find their identity in a world that often asks us to be someone else. Ira's journey from heartbreak and uncertainty to a place of profound self-love and faith is nothing short of inspiration. She reminds us that the strength we seek from the outside has been within us all along.

To my cousin, thank you for your courage. Thank you for your vulnerability. And thank you for this beautiful, thought-provoking, and uplifting book. Your voice is a gift, and I do not doubt that your story will empower and encourage countless others to embark on their own journeys of self-discovery and healing.

Avonda Ellison,
Owner at Laugh N' Learn Family Daycare

PREFACE

It is with deep admiration and profound respect that I write this foreword for a book that shares not just a story of survival but one of triumph. The journey you are about to explore is one of resilience, courage, and an unwavering belief that even in the darkest moments, hope's light never fades. This is the story of a woman who, despite overwhelming odds, stood tall through pain, heartache, and loss. Her story serves as a testament to the unbreakable strength that resides within when we cling to our faith.

In every chapter, you will see not only the trials she faced but also the beauty that came from her endurance. She did not just survive; she rose, often in ways she did not even realize were possible. Through the struggles, she has learned, grown, and trusted in God's promises.

I often reflect on Romans 8:18, which says, *"I consider that our present sufferings are not worth comparing with the glory that will be revealed in us."* This scripture encapsulates so much of what this book embodies—the transformation that happens when we surrender our pain to God and trust that the best is yet to come. This book is a testament to that promise.

You will also find that the book speaks to a truth found in Isaiah 43:19: *"See, I am doing a new thing! Now it springs up; do you not perceive it?"* Every page reveals how God can turn sorrow into joy, transform brokenness into strength, and create beauty in places we thought were beyond repair.

This book is more than just words on paper; it's a guide for anyone who has ever wondered whether their pain serves a purpose, whether their journey has significance, and whether their future holds anything but more heartache. To anyone who has asked, "What's next?" or "Is this all there is?"—this book will respond with the powerful truth that the best is yet to come.

In the words of Jeremiah 29:11, *"For I know the plans I have for you, declares the Lord, plans for welfare and not for evil, to give you a future and a hope."* And this, my dear friend, is exactly what this book embodies—the hope that God is still writing your story, and the next chapter is filled with purpose, peace, and promise.

As you turn the pages, remember this is more than just a book—it is a beacon of hope, a reminder of God's constant faithfulness, and an invitation to believe that your story, too, is just beginning. This book is essential for anyone who has faced trials, doubts, or fears, and for anyone who needs encouragement to keep moving forward. As you will discover in these pages, the best is not only ahead, but also already happening before you. May you be blessed, inspired, and reminded that nothing is ever wasted in God's hands.

Sisterly Love,

Lady Lisha Holloman
(Gilfield Baptist Church, Ivor, VA)

INTRODUCTION

In the Bible, there is a story in Genesis chapter 3 about Adam and Eve and what is considered the fall of mankind. In this biblical story, God instructed Adam and Eve to live freely in the Garden of Eden. The only thing He told them not to do was eat fruit from the tree of the knowledge of good and evil. While in the garden, the Bible states that a serpent approached Eve and began gaslighting her by twisting God's instructions about the rules for living in the garden. Let us pause for a moment and talk about what it means when someone is gaslighting you. You see, gaslighting is a form of psychological manipulation where someone subtly tries to make another person doubt their sanity, perception of reality, or memories. It is a tactic used to control and undermine the victim, often leading them to question their own thoughts and feelings. This is what the serpent did to Eve. This is why knowing who you are and having an identity is important.

The scripture goes on to say that the serpent came to Eve and said, "Yeah, I heard God told y'all not to eat from any of these trees in this garden."

Eve replied, "Nope, that is not what He said! He said we can eat from the trees, just not the one in the center of the garden." Eve told him that if they ate of that tree, God said they would surely die.

Here is where the gaslighting really starts. In verse four, the serpent slyly tells Eve, "Ye shall not surely die. See, what God knows is that the moment you eat from that tree, your eyes will be opened, and ye shall be as gods, knowing good and evil." Now, right here is where this heifer had God messed up. Instead of standing on business because she knew what God had instructed her to do, she went ahead and ate the forbidden fruit, then gave it to her husband, and he ate it as well.

Now, I want to share my own little two cents on

why I believe she ate the fruit. In verse six, it states that "When the woman saw that the tree was good for food, and that it was pleasant to the eyes, and a tree to be desired to make one wise, she took of the fruit thereof, and did eat, and gave also unto her husband with her and he did eat." I believe there were two separate reasons she chose to listen to the narcissistic serpent instead of God. The first reason was that it states she "saw" that the tree was pleasant to the eyes. Now, I do not know about you, but I am somewhat of a visual person. Something needs to look a certain way to catch my interest. This could be anything from a man to a plate of food. If it does not look right, it does not grab my attention. I know I am not the only one like this. This book is about being real and true to ourselves. She now had sight of the tree that was once talked about but not seen as desirable. She did not see the tree in this light until she was persuaded to do so. It's interesting how other people can make us doubt what we know is true. Why do we often consider others' opinions more trustworthy than our own understanding? I think it's because we want to fit in and be accepted. Choosing to go along with the crowd instead of standing by the truth and facts may seem crazy, but we do it anyway.

Reason number two is that she now desired the tree. Desire means to yearn for, wish for, or covet. So, Eve now desired the forbidden tree and its fruit. She took the fruit, ate it, and then gave it to her husband to eat. The moment they ate the fruit, the Bible says that their eyes were opened, and they immediately realized that they were naked. They hid from God when He sought them out in the garden because of that nakedness. When Eve ate that fruit, she changed her identity. What's crazy is that she also persuaded her husband to change his.

Here they were in the garden for however long, and not once did they have a desire to touch, look at, or eat the fruit from that tree. Suddenly, because someone told her to look at it from an unfamiliar perspective, she decided it was better to do that than to listen to God. Does this sound familiar to anyone yet?

Nope, not to me either. Sike! Now you know just as well as I do that this sounds just like our stubbornness.

Before eating the fruit, Adam and Eve were in a state of innocent obedience to God. Obedience was their identity and how they presented themselves to God. Afterward, their eyes were opened to the knowledge of good and evil, and they realized they were naked and felt shame. This marked the end of their innocence and their original identity. God created them to be innocent and pure; they did not know guilt or shame. They only saw themselves as God's perfect creation. After the disobedience, they took on the identities of guilt and shame. This changed how they viewed themselves and how God now views them. Where He once saw His perfect creation, He now saw disobedience, sin, and death.

This identity crisis not only changed the way God viewed them but also how He would view all of mankind. When they changed their identities, they also forced God to change His plans for them. This is what happens when we step out of God's will. Our identities change. We conform to the characteristics of our surroundings.

In this book, I will share my personal journey of how I lost my Christ-given identity and the steps I took to regain it. It details the highs and lows I faced while trying to discover who I was created to be and how to stay true to that without compromising or conforming to the world's version of who it needed me to be for acceptance. My prayer is that everyone who reads this leaves with a deeper understanding of who they are and why it is so important to never lose sight of that. I also pray it draws readers closer to God, knowing that He is the source of our true identities, which exist only in and through Him.

CHAPTER ONE

WHAT IN THE WORLD WILL I DO?

God, something feels off in this house, and I do not know what it is. I need You to show me what it is and give me guidance on how to fix it. God, I can sense something shifting, and I am praying that, no matter what it is, Your will be done. God, remove ANYTHING and EVERYTHING that is not meant to go with me into these next seasons of my life. I do not care what or who it is. Even if You must break my heart to save my life, break my heart but save my life, Lord.

This is a prayer I prayed one day in April 2024. I felt something was wrong, and I knew that only God could reveal and fix whatever it was. Honestly, I was not ready for what happened next or how quickly it happened. I asked God to please show me what was going on.

His response was, "Are you sure you want to know, daughter?"

I told Him, "Yes."

He asked the same question again, and I knew that whatever it was, it was about to change my life.

"I don't want you anymore. Actually, I never did. I am sorry, but I cannot fake it anymore, Ira. I never really wanted to marry you. I did it because I knew that was the only way I could continue to be with you to get what I wanted. When I met you, I was on the verge of losing everything… my house, my car, my children, and my job. You came along, with so much joy, and brought this light with you that I could not explain, but I knew I needed whatever it was you had in you. You were my way out of my current situation at that time. You were my escape. I used you. I was always going to leave you. I'm just mad that you were not more established, so I could have at least left with something. I did not gain anything from being married to you. I WANT A DIVORCE!"

These were the words spoken to me by my husband, the very next day after praying the prayer above and asking God to remove anyone and everything that did not belong in the next seasons of my life. After a brief period of silence, a scream erupted from my soul. My entire body started to shake. My voice cracked and trembled as I begged him to tell me what had happened and why he felt this way after 10 years together. "What did I do wrong? How can I change? What can I do better? I don't want a divorce. Why are you saying these things? Can we do therapy?"

He responded, "There is nothing here to save, Ira."

My whole world felt like it was slipping away from me. My chest felt tight, and I was struggling to breathe. *What am I supposed to do now?* This marked the start of a very painful journey in my life. I would have to undo everything I had spent the past 10 years building. I reminded him again that he was about to throw away an entire decade. He said he was tired of pretending to be something and someone he was not. He could no longer keep it up and knew he would eventually hate me if he stayed. He said he simply could not be the man I needed and was tired of trying to be.

"What am I supposed to do without you? Do you not understand the things I gave up for you? Do you not understand what I compromised? Are you just going to throw me away like I am nothing and walk away? You are a coward, and you stole my life from me. I cannot believe you are doing this. Please, let's just try therapy."

Everything this man did afterward showed me he meant every word he spoke. He did not care what he said to me or how he said it. He started staying out all night and through the next day. He continually reminded me that he was only there until I figured things out, but he was leaving, and I could not say anything to stop him. He told me I did not do anything to deserve what he was doing, but he just wanted to live his life and did not want to do it with me anymore.

I would go to bed crying at night and wake up crying. My heart was broken, and my life was falling apart. I sat on the edge of the bed one day, and in between sobs, I asked God what was happening and why. God said He was only answering the prayer I put before Him. I told Him I had no idea this is what was happening. This is what I felt in the pit of my stomach every time I walked in the house lately. Again, He stated, "You asked, and I answered."

Now, I am going to pause right here and tell you that if you are not serious about this prayer, please shut your mouth. When you tell God to have His way and allow His will to be done, that is exactly what happens. The problem with this is that we do not always like or agree with HIS WILL. So again, if you are not ready for some unexpected changes in life, do not pray this prayer. LOL!

I wanted God to fix it, but I wanted it done my way, not His. I thought He would fix us. I thought He would restore the broken marriage. Instead, He chose to remove what was hindering the restoration that was needed in me. I did not like it at first, but I knew it was necessary. It was not punishment, but an effort to save my life. I say it was an effort because only I could decide whether to obey what God was trying to do for me.

Everything in my life was uprooted. I had to move from my home. I had to change phone numbers because my old number was on my husband's phone plan. I had to change my emergency contacts on all my legal documents. Each time I had to make one of these changes, it felt like I lost another piece of myself. I felt so lost and abandoned. I just wanted things back to normal, even if normal was dysfunctional.

That's crazy, right? Isn't it crazy how we will stay in or run back to dysfunction just because it is normal or familiar? As humans, we prefer what is comfortable and familiar, even if it is unhealthy. The unknown can be intimidating, making the known feel less threatening. I was willing to choose to continue to be in a horrible situation for fear of being alone.

If you are in a situation like this, it is time to ask God for a way of escape. The longer you stay, the worse it will be when it finally ends. If He tells you to go, GO! Do not question it. Do not try to figure out the "what ifs." Just move when He says to move. Ask Him for a plan and resources to help you fund this new journey.

All I know is that I had to learn to trust Him in ways I never had before. I had to be patient and wait for Him to move on His time and do it His way. I became so frustrated and sometimes discouraged, but I had to wait. I wanted to trust Him to fix it, but I just wanted Him to hurry up and do it.

I remember when my kids and I were searching for a new place to live because I could no longer afford our current home after my husband left. We kept getting rejected because my credit wasn't in good enough shape. I kept praying and telling God how much I trusted Him to see us through. We had a deadline to move out of the old place, and we couldn't find a new one in time. We went to an apartment complex and were told that we were approved. We paid our deposits and completed all our paperwork, feeling very excited and relieved to finally stop looking. It looked like our new beginning was about to start, and we could finally relax a bit.

One day, while I was working, I received an email from the apartment complex stating that they had made a mistake and that we would no longer be getting the place. We were right back where we started. We were scrambling again, almost in panic mode, as our deadline to move out of the current place was rapidly approaching. My daughter and I used every free moment we had online and drove around looking for "for rent" signs. One day, we went out and decided to check a few more apartment complexes. We went to one and were told that we would definitely qualify and were given the steps to prepare for move-in.

We dotted every "I" and crossed every "T." We made sure all documents were turned in and signed on time. I sold my washer and dryer to cover the security deposit and first month's rent. We were given an apartment unit number and a move-in date. We signed our lease online and waited for the rental office to contact us to schedule a walk-through and hand over our keys.

Days went by, and we did not hear anything from the complex. One day, we received an email stating that our unit would be changed and that we needed to sign the lease for that unit. They sent us the documents online, and we signed them that day. Something was off. I kept telling my daughter that something did not feel right. She tried to reassure me by telling me that I was just having anxiety due to the other setbacks that we had. But I knew that was not it.

While we were leaving the rental office for the third time, trying to contact them to find out what was going on with the move, I started praying. I needed God to reveal what was happening and what we needed to do. God told me to tell her to drive down a certain street. I told her, and we began to talk while driving. In our chatting, we drove down the street God had suggested, but we were so caught up in our conversation that we kept on rolling and ended up somewhere totally different. When we got home, my phone rang. It was the rental office telling me they had reviewed our applications again and decided not to allow us to move in after all.

I was angry. I fussed at the lady for giving us false hope. I asked about getting a refund for the deposit I gave them. She said it would take 30 days to return. I told her I needed it sooner, just in case I found a new place; I would need that money as a deposit. She said she would try to get it expedited because the mistake was theirs, not ours.

At this point, we had 14 days before we had to be out. We had planned to put our belongings in storage and move into a hotel until we figured things out. I prayed every day, telling God that no matter what, I trusted Him to come through. God was quiet. I needed Him to say something.

God, what am I supposed to do? They are counting on me to make something happen for us. God remained silent. One day, my sister texted me and said that one of her co-workers was riding down the street when they saw a house-for-rent sign. She sent me the number and told me to call the people right away. I did exactly that. The guy on the phone told me two other candidates were interested in the house, but I could still apply. He explained what was needed to be approved, including a certain credit score. Well, that already disqualified me. I was about to tell him, "Never mind," when he said, "Just apply and come by tomorrow to see the place, we can go from there."

The next day, my daughter and I met the guy. When we got there, he started showing us the house. It took me about 10 minutes to figure out this house was on that same street God had told me to ride down the day my daughter and I were out looking for a place. I whispered to her, "This is it." She told me she felt it when we walked in but didn't want to say anything until we got in the car.

The guy showing us around let us back into the living room and started talking about our application, saying it was just one other candidate and me. He said, "Here is the dilemma: you have the income, but your credit is not so good. The other candidate has the credit, but they are stating they do not know when they would be able to have the security deposit and first month's rent."

As I started to speak, God said, "Tell him your story. Tell him what you are going through right now." I was a bit embarrassed, but I was obedient. He told me he would speak with the actual landlord and get back with us in a few days. You'd better know they were the longest few days of my entire life.

I received a call saying we had the house and needed to pay the deposit immediately. The deposit was $1,700.00, and the first month's rent was the same. That totaled $3,400.00, which had to be paid in less than five days. We had the deposit, which I paid the very next day. However, we still did not have the first month's rent. Again, I panicked a little.

I told God that He was the one who led us to this house, so I was putting the money issue in His hands and letting Him figure it out. Let me just go on the record to say that God never has to figure out anything. He already knows the outcome because He orchestrated the plan from the beginning.

We had 24 hours left before meeting the landlord to pay the first month's rent, sign the lease, and get the keys. After experiencing two traumatic incidents during this process, anxiety started to creep in. Mainly because we were $1,000 short and only had 24 hours to fix it. I had no idea where to get the money, and payday was still seven days away.

God, what in the world am I going to do? God told me to go to sleep. I prayed, listened to my worship music, and went to bed. I woke up early and told God that, outside of a miracle from Him, I did not know what we would do. We had to meet the lady at noon, and it was already 8:00 a.m. I got up and got dressed. My daughter called and asked what we were going to do. I told her, "Baby, we are going to trust God because at this point, we have no other choice."

As I was taping up the last few boxes of the things I packed in my bedroom, my phone rang. It was my mom. She said, "Hey, Pie!" Pie is my nickname given to me by my grandma when I was a baby, because my face was fat. SMH! I greeted my mom and asked her what she was up to. She asked me if I had ever found a way to get $1,000.00. I told her no, but I was trusting God. She said, "I am in your yard, come open the door." When I opened the door, she told me to open my hand. I did, and she placed $1,000 in my hand and said, "Let's go get you and these kids this house!" The way I praised God in that living room was something serious.

When we pulled up to the house, she said, "You know, I passed by this house the other day and thought about you." She said, "I told the Lord to send you a house for you and the kids. I had no clue this was the one you were going to be getting."

When we got inside and spoke with the landlord, I gave her the money, and she gave me the lease to sign. She looked at me and said, "Do you want to know what made me choose you?"

I said, "Yes, ma'am."

She said the guy's name who showed my daughter and me the house and said he told me your story.

Your story is my story. I went through that with my daughter. I know how that feels. I know what it is like. She said God had told her that I needed a second chance. She said, "When I was in your position, someone did it for me, so I have to do it for you." She hugged me and gave me the keys to our new beginning.

I told you this story because throughout all of this, I kept asking God, "What in the world will I do?" God was speaking, even in His silence. He was saying, "What you should do is trust me even when I am silent. Just know that I am working on your behalf throughout it all. He kept sending me to Psalm 46:10, which says, *"Be still and know that I am God."* God was trying to get me to stop focusing on my problems and to acknowledge that He is the solution.

Life is full of ups, downs, and uncertainties. Our only job is to trust that the one who created us and this crazy thing called life is in complete control. He will not let us be overwhelmed by the worries of this world. He has already written our ending; we just need to keep going through it all.

CHAPTER TWO

FACING THE REALITY OF MY FEARS

Job 3:25 says, *"For the thing which I greatly feared is come upon me, and that which I was afraid of is come unto me."* This statement reflects Job's experience of suffering and the fulfillment of his deepest anxieties. Job's words highlight how his worst fears—losing his family, possessions, and health—became reality. He also feared negative opinions from others, which proved true. The verse captures the idea that what one dreads most can indeed happen. If you read the book of Job, it details the events of Job's life and tells the story of a man whom the Bible describes as upright and just.

It describes how Job lost his wife, children, cattle, servants, friends, and everything else that represented his life. He feared this loss, and then it became reality. It teaches us that sometimes we face hardships in life, even when we try to do everything right. That fear shows no favoritism, and everyone carries some kind of fear, whether we want to admit it or not. Sometimes those fears come true. When this happens, it can leave us questioning our own lives, actions, and our relationship with God.

Fears, as intimidating as they can be, can help you focus. They also help you identify your position relative to what you are sensing. They bring all your senses into the present moment. While fear can act as a barrier, it can also serve as a powerful trigger for spiritual awakening. When we confront our fears, we often uncover our deepest desires and motivations. This prompts us to develop qualities like courage, resilience, and self-compassion. The next step is to face them.

At first, the worst part of having fears is facing them head-on. This means actually admitting that this specific thing causes fear and that it needs to be addressed. I have a good friend who is terrified of water bugs. I mean, she almost goes into a state of shock when she sees them. One day, she was entering a house when she happened to see one because of all the rain, and the area around the home was infested with large insects when it rained heavily. She ran out of the house and jumped into her car. She was so terrified that every noise she heard, she thought it was a water bug moving. It got so bad that she almost wrecked her car.

This kind of fear is almost debilitating. It keeps you from moving forward. It keeps you from accomplishing things. Now, she is afraid to enter that house without someone else being present to check it for any signs of water bugs, dead or alive. This kind of fear can keep you stuck for years, decades even. I often wonder what would happen if it clicks within her that the bugs are actually more afraid of her than she is of them? I can only imagine the type of satisfaction she would get every time she stomps on one, killing it. Killing the very thing that once paralyzed her. The joy that would fill her heart knowing this thing no longer has power or control over her or her life.

I always bore the burden of feeling like I was not enough, which ingrained a fear of rejection in me. I was so afraid of being rejected that I would do anything to avoid it. Sometimes, I would sabotage things in my life if it even seemed like they were going wrong. I would not even give it time or a chance. I would run and move on to the next thing, then make a million excuses for why I had to walk away from it. It sounds crazy, but I feared being rejected that much.

I had to learn the hard way that rejection is part of life. Also, I realized that rejection is not always a dreadful thing. Sometimes it even saves your life. Can you imagine what would happen to some of us if God did not allow certain people and things to reject us? If He let us have everything and everybody we wanted or thought we needed. I do not know about you, but when I think about the people who told me "No" or walked away from me in my past, I thank God and am grateful that He blocked or removed them.

My fear of rejection was due to my identity crisis. I did not know who I was. I had to learn that rejection from a person did not change who I am. It did not define what type of person, mother, wife, friend, etc., that I am. But if I am being truthful, it made me second-guess myself in those roles. It made me go overboard trying to please people, no matter what it cost me. You can imagine how exhausting this was.

I remember my very first job as an executive director. I was excited to finally do what I had worked so hard to achieve. It was one of the best feelings in the world. I jumped into the role headfirst and learned quickly. My preceptor told me I was the best mentee she had ever mentored. I was accomplishing things in that building that had never been done before. I was reaching goals that had never been reached and keeping the budget out of the negative. I helped build a solid team and reduced turnover from 86% to 38%. That was also the first for that building. I led my team to achieve the best state survey the building had ever experienced since opening. We even made the Forbes and Wall Street best business list.

Imagine my surprise when I was called into the boss's office and received a raise. I was also asked to help out at other buildings. My preceptor and I would travel to different locations to assist with inspections or fix issues for reinspection. I began receiving calls from corporate, telling me I was a valuable asset to the company and that they saw a very bright future for me with the organization.

One day, while finishing a complaint survey, I was called to my boss's office. When I arrived, my preceptor was there with our boss, and she was crying. I did not know what was going on, but suddenly my entire body reacted to the tension in that room. I felt a huge knot in my throat, which made it almost impossible to swallow. The silence in that room was deafening. It seemed like everyone wanted to speak, yet no one said a word. My boss then began to tell me how much she appreciated me and how much the place had grown since I was hired. She discussed my progress across everything, from the budget to staffing.

Then it happened. The other shoe dropped. She stated the corporation was making cuts and that there were three executive directors in the community, and they needed to remove one. She said we must fire you today. I immediately started trying to explain to her why they were making a mistake by firing me and whether there was anything I could do to make them reconsider. She looked me in the face and told me I had done absolutely nothing wrong, and it was just politics. That is just how things go sometimes, unfortunately. Then she told me I could work out my 30 days, but I had to write a letter worded as if I were resigning from my position. I later learned that this was to cover them so I would not sue them for wrongful termination.

Now, let me get this straight. I provided them

with some of the best budgets, surveys, and staffing they had ever seen, and they just discarded me like garbage. Then they had the nerve to blame me and make it my fault. After that, I never spent a full year in any other building as an executive director. As soon as things started to seem off, no matter how well things were going, I would leave. No one else would ever enjoy the satisfaction of beating me and throwing me away as if I did not matter. Self-sabotage became my new identity, along with the fear of rejection.

I didn't care to fight for anything anymore. In my mind, I thought I could just walk away and start fresh. A good friend once told me that doing that was one of the most foolish things she had ever heard. She said some things are worth staying and fighting for. Stop being afraid and FIGHT back. I heard her, but I just didn't have it in me to do so. I was so exhausted from adopting so many characteristics and identities that I thought I needed to be accepted by others and avoid rejection. I lacked the strength to do anything else.

Fear is a basic human emotion triggered by perceived danger or threat and characterized by physical and mental responses. It acts as a survival tool, preparing the body for "fight, flight, or freeze" reactions. Although fear is a natural and often helpful emotion, it can become a problem when it is excessive, irrational, or overwhelming.

My fear was problematic because it was truly debilitating. My fear of failure caused me to miss out on many opportunities and connections. This fear of rejection kept me in a relationship with the wrong man for nine years longer than I should have. I knew in the first year that this relationship wouldn't be fruitful, but not wanting to face the fact that I made the wrong choice, I kept going. As the years went by, it only got worse, and my fear of losing it grew stronger. Isn't that crazy? It was obvious it needed to end, but in my mind, ending meant rejection, and I was not willing to go through that again. So, I kept compromising parts of myself, which caused me to lose my identity further—chipping away pieces of who I was to avoid facing what had to happen.

Eventually, what I feared most happened, and there was nothing I could do but confront it head-on. I was about to go into a 12-round bout with fear, rejection, and self-sabotage. The odds were stacked against me. I was afraid to confront these things, but had no other choice, since they were staring me right in the face. This was going to be hard. I needed some help. I needed God!

Facing the reality of your fears means acknowledging them, understanding their origins, and taking intentional steps to confront them. I had to realize that fear is a natural human experience and nothing to be ashamed of. I had to learn how to identify and learn from my fears.

I had to ask myself where these fears originated. Are they based on past experiences, negative self-beliefs, or societal pressures? Mine was somewhere between them all. See, learning how to analyze my fears helped me to reframe and challenge them. I had to ask myself whether the thoughts that came along with my fears were realistic. Are they helping me in any way?

I am learning what triggers my fears and why. One thing I realized was that what triggered them was the fear of rejection. I then had to understand where that originated from. I repeatedly went over in my mind where it could have started. What age? What life event? Who even? I did the only thing left to do; I asked God to show me.

While spending time with God, He began to show me where I had started to place things in the space where He used to be. He revealed the root of my identity crisis and the origin of my fear. He showed me how I got here and what it would take to lift me out of this situation. It actually stemmed from trying to depend on my own strength to handle the daily busyness of life. I stopped fearing God and started believing I could control the narratives and move the pieces as I wanted.

I followed what I felt was right in situations

instead of always seeking His guidance. God showed me that if I let go of my need to control, I wouldn't be so afraid of what might happen if things do not work out, because my trust would be in the one who controls the outcome. *"For God has not given us a spirit of fear, but of power and of love and of a sound mind."* (2 Timothy 1:7 ESV) He told me I was driving myself crazy trying to avoid rejection in situations I created, where the only possible outcome would be rejection.

Fears are natural, but giving in to them can definitely be controlled by trusting God. Being honest about our deepest fears and anxieties allows Him to reveal their true nature and origin and provides us with a strategy to overcome them.

CHAPTER THREE

THE SILENT SHAME

The word shame is defined as a painful feeling of humiliation or distress that arises from becoming aware of having done something wrong or foolish. Yep, go ahead and read it again before you roll your eyes and realize that the definition was calling you out. LOL! That's exactly what I did. Fighting rejection and this identity crisis I was going through made me do something crazy and impulsive.

Two months after my husband left, I was not in a good headspace. I felt used, rejected, useless, and unwanted. I was doing everything I could to push myself every day to do what needed to be done. Then I would get into bed, pull the covers over my head, and sob until I fell asleep. I did this day after day. I was broken and just wanted to feel something other than pain and rejection.

One day, after getting out of the shower, I sat on the toilet and started sobbing. I cried so hard that my nose began to run, and I ended up vomiting. My whole body was aching. I had the worst headache I have ever had. My vision blurred. My heart was pounding rapidly. I was experiencing chest pain and had difficulty breathing. This ordeal was really taking a toll on both my mental and physical health.

I lay on my bed and sobbed until it was time for work. I put on my work clothes and headed out the door. Once I got to work, I wiped my eyes in the car, put a smile on my face, and greeted my coworkers on my way to the time clock. Isn't it crazy how quickly we can switch gears to handle what needs to be handled? It was as if I were a robot turning myself on and off as needed.

One day, I had enough. I was angry, and I could no longer hide it. I stood in the middle of my bedroom floor, flaring my arms. I was yelling and crying. I asked God why He would allow this to happen to me. *Why did You sit back and let this man do this to me? I was a good wife to him. I was not the type of wife I saw my mom be. I was not the type of wife I saw others around me be. I honored that man. I loved him. I cared for him. I did what You told me to do in your word concerning my husband and marriage. I do not understand. I feel like you let me down, God. Why? Why do I have to go through this?*

When I tell you God gut-punched me so hard I lost my breath. God told me in a very stern voice, "Don't you dare blame me for your mess, girl." He explained that I was in this identity crisis because of myself, and He had absolutely nothing to do with it. He told me that if I had stayed where He had me, that man would not have been able to find me. He said I was not even on that man's radar because he could not see that far up. He said, "Ira, you moved, not me.

You came down to where he was. You put yourself on his radar. You allowed yourself to be seen and found by him. You left me out of it. You did not consult me about him. You did not ask me if he needed to be in your life or if you belonged in his. You allowed your loneliness and desperation to lead you to where you are now. You said he was the one. You kept telling yourself this man was your husband, even though he showed you every sign he was not suitable for you. You did not ask me before you stood there and exchanged those vows. Let's be honest, he never valued you. He never really respected you. You caught him in lie after lie, yet you still convinced yourself that I sent him to you. Why would I, the one who created you for nothing less than greatness, give you anything but greatness in return? DON'T YOU EVER AGAIN BLAME ME FOR YOUR MOVING OUT OF POSITION. You moved! I didn't!"

Do you feel that? Yeah, that feeling you get inside after reading that. Yep, that's how I felt. I sat there staring into space. I couldn't even form a thought in my own mind. I was speechless. God had just, as the young folks say, clocked my tea really bad. He shut me down. He had to make sure I knew that I was not going to get delusional and act like I didn't know how I got into this mess or whose fault it was.

He told me I needed to allow Him to reveal who I was created to be. He ministered to me, explaining how He made me different, and everyone around me could see it. I was the only one unable to see or understand how He made me and set me apart. He said that I was so preoccupied with trying to figure out why He called me that, I could not look past the doubt I had created for myself. I had convinced myself I wasn't worthy, so I accepted less and called it good. He said that not just anyone could have me, and I could not have just anyone.

It took me a few days to get myself together from that whooping God had just given me. And although I do not want to admit it, it was well deserved. *Who in the world did I think I was blaming God for some mess I did to myself because I didn't know who I was?*

Once I accepted what was said to me, the silent shame set in.

I was ashamed of myself. I felt sick to my stomach again, but this time for a different reason. This happened because of me. I did this to myself. I allowed it by failing to maintain the posture and position that God had placed me in. Although my husband did what he did, my identity crisis was the fuel that lit the fire. This shifted my mindset. It took my focus off what was done to me and put it on how I was supposed to fix it.

How do I escape this place of shame? For months, I have been beating myself up. Every time I try to enter God's presence, shame takes over, and I feel unworthy again. I start to avoid social interactions, fearing others will judge or reject me. I begin to hide out, which triggers my anxiety. My shame leads me to believe the people around me see me as a failure, which makes me retreat even more.

It took me a few more months before I realized that God did not call me out to shame me. He is too good a father ever to do that. He called me out so that I could recognize God's grace and forgiveness. I had to replace shame-based thoughts with His truths and seek vulnerability with safe individuals. I started this process by confessing my sins. I asked for His forgiveness for removing myself from His arch of safety. I then had to train myself to accept God's forgiveness. I then focused on my identity in Christ as a forgiven and loved child of God.

He just wanted me to know He loved me too much for me not to know who I was in Him. The Bible says in Hebrews 12:6, *"For whom the Lord loves He chastens, and scourges every son whom He receives."* He corrected me because He loves me. This allowed me to accept my new identity in Christ. It let me know that my past mistakes do not define me, and neither do they define you.

I started seeking God more. I became intentional about spending time with Him and asking Him to show me every character flaw that contributed to my identity crisis. I searched the scriptures and found every single one that spoke life into me. I did this so I had something to fight the negative and recurring thoughts of shame that would creep up every now and then.

The next thing I did was ask God to send me someone I could share my most vulnerable secrets with. Someone who would not judge but would help, pray, and guide me through this journey of self-discovery. And you better know, He did just that. This person helped me realize that I should not try to compare my journey to anyone else's and that I should give both God and myself time. I should have patience, knowing that with persistence and continuous seeking of God, I would come out better on the other side of this journey.

I learned to accept my imperfections. This helped me stop feeling the need to compromise because I did not feel good enough. I would literally stand in front of the mirror and tell myself that I was good enough. I said it until I started to believe that I am good enough just the way I am. Any changes that need to happen,

God will reveal, and as I submit to His will, He will prune the areas that need correction and updating.

Zephaniah 3:19 says this about shame. It says, *"Behold, at that time I will undo all that afflict thee: and I will save her that halteth, and gather her that was driven out; and I will get them praise and fame in every land where they have been put to shame."* Right here is where we can rejoice. God never meant for us to live in a place of guilt or shame. That is not our identity. Remember that is the identity that Adam and Eve took on in the garden after disobeying God's command. Since they messed it up and caused that to be the identity of mankind, God sent Jesus to rescue us from that and restore our identities to their original form.

I would like to end this chapter with a prayer.

> *God, I thank you that in Christ, I am a new creation. The old (**insert your name here**) has gone, the new (**insert your name here**) has come. I choose*

to identify with my new self, not with my past sins or failures. Lord, I embrace my brand-new identity as your beloved child and creation, redeemed and forgiven through the blood of your son, Jesus. Help me to live in the reality of this truth. I declare that I am not defined by the mistakes I have made in the past or what others say about me. My true identity is in Christ, and I am chosen, royal, and holy. God, help me to see myself as your masterpiece whom you created for a unique plan and purpose. I pray that you reveal the talents and qualities you have placed inside of me and that I only strive to use them for your glory. Help me to embrace being made unique and not to feel the need to compare myself to anyone else. Allow your Holy Spirit to reveal to me the lies I have believed about my self-worth.

Give me the strength and power to cast them down. I reject and cast down every attempt of the enemy to distort my true identity in Christ, and in this, I will no longer be defined by insecurity, self-doubt, or shame. Help me to hear only your voice and follow your guidance in every situation from this day forward. Lord, I dedicate my life to you and choose to follow you wholeheartedly according to your word. In Jesus' name, Amen!

CHAPTER FOUR

LOOK WHO I FOUND

I'm a DC and Marvel fan. Superman is one of my favorite DC Comics characters. Superman was born on a planet called "Krypton." Krypton was about to be destroyed, so his parents sent him to Earth as a baby to escape the planet's destruction. He lands in Smallville and is adopted by the Kents. His earthly parents named him Clark Kent.

Superman possessed unique powers such as superhuman strength, X-ray vision, heat vision, superhuman speed, superhuman sight, flight, healing factor, and telepathy. Although he had these abilities, he had to hide them to maintain the appearance of being an ordinary human. Whenever a crime took place, Superman would find a telephone booth somewhere in the city. In that booth, he would change out of his regular clothes and into his superhero gear. He would fight the crime and then reenter the same telephone booth to change back into his street clothes.

Only a few people knew his true identity. That's what this chapter covers. It marks the moment I realized who Ira truly was—it revealed my real self and my true powers. In discovering this, I understood I had a long journey of self-discovery ahead. At this point, I am ready to embrace my flaws with Ira the imposter, so I can later reemerge and become Ira—the complete and authentic version.

I used the story of Superman because it provides the best example I could think of regarding an identity crisis. You might be wondering why I said Superman was experiencing an identity crisis. Well, let's take a closer look at his life, and you will clearly understand why I said what I did.

Remember when I told you that whenever there was talk of a crime, Clark Kent would find a phone booth and transform into Superman to fight the bad guys? Well, what if I told you that Clark Kent was actually an imposter? You might wonder how. He was an imposter because he was using Superman's identity. Yes, Superman was his real, true self once he took off his street clothes. Clark Kent was who he had to be to be accepted by the world he lived in. He walked around under a false identity because the world could not accept him for who he was. They could not accept him at full strength, so he had to dumb himself down and become someone else to fit in and gain acceptance from the world and his peers.

I can only imagine how disheartening it must have been to have all those special abilities and to hide them behind a pair of bifocals and suspenders. Why couldn't he just be SUPERMAN? Why was it easier for the world to accept the counterfeit instead of the original? I believe that his authentic self would have intimidated people, so they would have found every probable reason why he did not need to be different, to be more like the rest of us.

That's exactly where I was. I had conformed so much throughout my life to be who everyone else needed me to be that I had no clue who Ira really was. I became who my children needed me to be to serve them. So, I learned to like what they liked and dislike what they disliked. I became who my husband needed me to be to fulfill my role as his wife. So, I pushed away the things I liked and that defined me, and I picked up the things he liked and disliked. I became who my employer needed me to be to be productive at work. When I say, "I became," I mean I let go of myself to be the person everyone else could accept in the various roles I played.

The problem arose when my middle son was preparing to graduate from high school. It hit me that I only had one more child to graduate, and he would soon be an adult. After sacrificing so much of who I was to become who they needed me to be, I wondered where that left me. I got scared because at that moment, I felt like I might lose some of my purpose and a big part of my identity.

The fear intensified when my husband, who had just sat down with me the night before planning our five-year vow renewal, looked me in the face and told me he did not want to be married to me anymore and wanted a divorce. This news came a month before our anniversary. I went to work one day, and when I came home, he was gone. I was overwhelmed with so many emotions. A thousand thoughts and fears flooded my mind. The fear wasn't about being alone; I've experienced that before. The fear was simply of the unknown.

Who am I outside of being my children's primary caretaker (mom)? Who would I be now if I were no longer this man's wife? I lived my life so effortlessly in those roles, and in that space, I had no identity without them. Please don't think for a second that I am telling you not to be all that you have to be in your home with your children and spouse. What I am saying is to make sure you also have your own identity. Know what you like outside of them. Know what you dislike outside of them. What things bring you joy, etc.? You must know who you are in the midst of being who everyone around you needs you to be.

One day, while praying and writing in my prayer journal, I asked God some questions. I had a few things I was pondering and needed Him to clarify for me. The first question I asked was, "Why did He create me like this?" Why did He give me such a big, loving heart and nature, but not allow me to experience this kind of love in return? *God, why am I quick to have compassion on those who hurt me, to the point where I try to understand their reasons for what they did? Why am I so quick to forgive and move past it? What did I do to deserve not being loved and cared for properly? Why am I not good enough for them? Why is it so easy for people to walk away from me?* At this point, I guess God got tired of my kindergarten rants, so He simply said, "Ira, IT'S YOU. It was and has been you all along." I sat in silence, confused and a little bit mad, if I can be honest.

Here I am asking Him a straightforward question, and He is here talking about it's me!! *What's me?* Baby, God used His loud voice to tell my hips to calm down and listen.

Me: "YES, SIR." I shut right up and listened. Chile, I might think I'm bad, but when it comes to God, I ain't no fool. Has God ever had to use His daddy voice on you? If not, be grateful because I was shaken to my core. I mean, voice trembling while talking to Him and all. I mean scared, SCARED!

After I regained my senses, I listened as God began to speak to me in one of the softest, gentlest tones I had ever heard from Him. He knew that once He had my full attention, I no longer needed the stern "Big" voice daddy, but the gentle one. The kind that corrects you but then gives you a hug and a kiss on the forehead afterward. And He was right. This was the daddy I needed at that moment.

He said to me, "Ira, I am going to answer your questions with a few of my own. What is stopping you from being kind to yourself? What is stopping you from loving yourself with the same level of love that you so easily give to others? What if you woke up every day ready to show yourself the compassion you extend to others? What if you celebrated and encouraged yourself as you do with others? What if you pushed yourself as hard as you push for others? What if you took care of yourself the way you care for others? What is wrong with you that you can't see that you are more than capable of being loved the same way you love others? You can do it for yourself. I put my love inside of you, that's why I told you that it was always you!"

The more I thought about these questions, the worse that empty feeling grew in my stomach. He asked me how I expected someone to give me something I had never felt worthy enough to give myself. "There is no way I created you to love the way you do, and it was only supposed to be passed out to others, but not poured onto you by you."

God said to me, "You asked me why it is that no one has ever loved me the way I loved them." Y'all, His response to this blew my mind.

Are y'all ready for this? Homeboy said, and yes, I did say homeboy because that's the kind of relationship me and big "G" have. LOL! "The reason you have never received that kind of love in return is that the person I created to love you was so busy trying to prove her love to everyone else that SHE (me) didn't realize she was created to love herself, just like everyone else was loved by her. Ira, IT WAS ALWAYS YOU! You have everything inside of you to give "YOU" everything you need. You have me, but it is you that you are looking for. Ira, YOU NEED YOU!"

My dear readers, it was as if He had flipped a switch inside me because all of a sudden, I jumped up, ran to my mirror, and burst out laughing. I started smiling from ear to ear. I grabbed some clothes, a washcloth, and a towel, then jumped in the shower. After I was dressed, I combed my hair, put on makeup and earrings, and sprayed myself with perfume. I began tidying up my room to make it more organized. Something shifted inside me. I started to worship God like never before. I began thanking Him for creating me with such a big, loving nature. Thank you, God, for allowing me to be your example of love and compassion. Thank you, God, for allowing me to be your example of grace. Thank you, God, for creating me in your image and giving me my own unique identity. I had a "THANK YOU GOD" fit in the bedroom.

I ran back to the mirror and burst out laughing again. I started singing, then I even began to dance a little. There was a joy inside me that I hadn't known existed. I yelled at the top of my lungs,

"GODDDDDDDDDDD, IT WAS ALWAYS ME"!
Then I went right back to praising Him. For the first time in my life, I saw the Ira that was lost and hidden behind the trauma, pain, busyness, and more. I saw God, and He allowed me to see ME.

But what I really want you to pay close attention to is how my words shifted. They shifted from "God, why" to "God, thank you." I no longer had any questions. I now had motivation—motivation to BECOME. Become what, you may ask? To become me. That's why this chapter is entitled "LOOK WHO I FOUND." I was at the beginning of my journey to find myself. Oh, and guess what? There is no fear. This journey is a blank canvas, and I am ready to create, develop, and design. God will give a strategy, and I will simply obey.

From there, I grabbed a journal and started jotting down my likes and dislikes. I then highlighted the ones I took on to play the various roles in life. Guess what? I was left with only about four likes that were my own. Oh, and that dislike list looked like a rainbow because so many of them were highlighted. Turns out, Ira did not like or even care for over half of that list.

What now? Now I pray and ask God to help me find my true self. Please be aware that during this phase, some people may get upset when you realize you're no longer interested in things you used to enjoy. They might say, "You used to like it," or ask, "Oh, so you're brand new now, huh?" This is the moment to ask God for boldness and strength. Boldness to tell them that yes, you used to like it, but it no longer excites you. And the strength to not feel guilty for choosing yourself. I do not want anything that resembles that fake version of me.

I remember reconnecting with my husband because I thought it was better to be with him when I wanted some adult time, rather than being out here in these streets. That was the worst decision I ever made. We started talking about divorce, and I asked him if he was so sure he was done with the marriage, why was he still holding on to the divorce papers? I told him I felt like he was holding me hostage. At that moment, I sat up on the bed and told him to take me home. I told him this would not happen again, and I needed him to please turn in those papers. He looked at me and said he did not know why he was still holding on to them, or even if he wanted to turn them in. I got dressed, walked over to the mirror, and looked at myself.

I pointed at myself and said, "Girl, NO. Ira, don't you do it. This is not where you're supposed to be. You don't even want to be here for real." He asked me what I was doing. I told him that I was reminding myself that it was always me. I wouldn't go back to what tried to break and destroy me. I lost so much of myself and wasn't willing to give any more to what didn't deserve me. Listen to what I said next. I LOVE IRA TOO MUCH TO SETTLE FOR LESS THAN EVER AGAIN. When we pulled up to my house, I opened the door and said goodbye.

He looked at me and then dropped his head. He said, "I thought you loved me, Ira."

I looked him straight in the eyes and said, "I do love you, but I love Ira more. Also, what I realized while lying in that bed beside you was that this version of me loves you, but I no longer like you. I wish you the best, but you have to stand by the decision you made."

Normally, I would repeat that scene in my head repeatedly and feel guilty, even though I was standing up for myself. That's what the old me would have done. But this new version of me wasn't backing down from standing up for herself. I still love him, but I know I deserve better than what he has to offer.

I recently met a guy. He was a Christian man who lived his life for Christ and had no problem letting anyone know that he loved Him. He was very easy on the eyes. Yes, he was fine, FINE. LOL! He owned several businesses and was a true gentleman. He told me that something felt different when he spoke to me, but he just couldn't quite figure out what it was. He kept saying, "I prayed to God to meet someone like you." This just seems too good to be true. The old Ira would have tried to convince him that this was from God and that we should pursue this.

One night, while on the phone, he said, "I just don't want to be fooled because people pretend well."

I told him, laughing, that I had lived that first-hand and would never do it again.

He asked how I would weed out those who were not who they claimed to be.

I told him, "I ask God to show me." I said, "I will not move until He reveals the answer. Whatever He says, I go with it. I do not second-guess or question it. I just go with it."

I told him to ask God about me. "Tell Him to show you Ira. I may be able to hide from you in my natural state, but the spirit always reveals the truth." I told him that I had already put his name before God and was waiting for Him to reveal his true character and motives.

As the days went on, we spoke less and less. This was after I asked God to reveal his true intentions, by the way. While on the phone, I told him I liked him but was waiting to hear from God. He told me he liked me too, but he was trying to figure out how much because I didn't look like the woman he normally went after. I paused, smiled, and said, "You'd better go with what God tells you, sir."

I smiled because at that moment, I knew something he didn't know. I knew I had overcome the fear of rejection this time. I wasn't afraid of him saying he didn't like me or that I didn't match the women he usually dates. I wasn't worried about everything not working out. I felt confident and content in myself at that moment. I saw God at that moment. God told me during prayer that the man He has for me will love everything about me, and he wouldn't compare me to anyone else because, to him, I was enough just the way God created me.

As time went on, the conversation slowed down. It got to the point that I didn't even think about him until he texted. One day, I informed him that I was not going to continue with this here-and-there follow-up text situation. I told him I had enough friends and was not interested in being his. "You are telling me you still need to figure out how much you like me is only your way of trying to keep me holding on until you push whatever agenda you are trying to push. Well, that stops here. I am not that girl anymore. I know who I am! I have no time, nor will I make any time for unfruitful connections."

At this point, I decided I would rather be hated for who I am than loved for pretending to be someone I'm not. I am no longer the woman who accepts anything just to be accepted. Both God and I have agreed that I deserve better, and until He sends someone worthy of being in my space and breathing my air, I will treat myself with kindness. I am finally giving myself the time, attention, energy, love, grace, forgiveness, and peace that I deserve. I'm no longer looking outside of God and myself for those things. If you're one of those people waiting for certain things to be reciprocated, STOP WAITING. The person God created to do that has already arrived. It's you! It has always been YOU!

CHAPTER FIVE

STARTING FROM SCRATCH

Most of the time, we don't want to face the reality of endings and cycles because we dislike facing the fact that we now must start over. Yep, we must start from scratch. We need to rebuild, brick by brick and layer by layer. This is scary, but it can also be maddening at times. I was watching an episode of *Divorce Court* one day, and there was a lady there with a man she clearly needed to run from as fast as possible, and it needed to happen quickly. The more evidence showed that this man clearly did not want, need, or respect this woman in any way, the more she begged him to please stay with her.

The judge repeatedly told her she was capable of doing better and that she was better than that. The woman kept saying it had been 16 years, and even though it had all been bad, she did not want to start over. She kept telling the judge how unfair it was to have to give up everything and start over. Every time she said, "But I just don't want to start over," she cried. She was afraid of the unknown.

The guy stood off to the side, smiling the most demonic-looking smile I had ever seen. Then he said to the judge, "See your honor, it doesn't matter what I do, she ain't going nowhere." I sat there with my eyes wide and my mouth agape, listening to this smug rascal say these things. The more he spoke, the more the woman cried. It seemed crazy to everyone in the audience and the judge. Why wouldn't she just let him go? The answer is simple. She just did not know who she was. She did not realize she had the power to change that situation in an instant. She was so caught up in how much she did not want to let go of all the sacrifices she made for him in this going-nowhere relationship that she did not realize she sacrificed her own identity, self-worth, self-esteem, integrity, and peace for a relationship that was designed from the beginning to take more than it would ever give back.

Starting over, no matter how necessary, can also be the most frightening and difficult thing even to consider. I was a little afraid of this at first. Before I invited God in, I kept trying to figure out how to do it. How was I going to start over? What does starting over entail? Where would I even begin?

Duh! Girl, you start where it all began. You start with God. That's what I told myself. He just showed you that you already have everything you need inside you to accomplish what must be done. Ask Him for a strategy. So, here is where I tell you to ask God for guidance. Begin with prayer, clearly stating your need for direction. Seek God's wisdom through His word, prayer, and by paying attention to His leading via impressions or peace. Also, be open to receiving the strategy in different ways, like through a dream, a prophetic word, or a practical insight. Ask Him how to start. Ask Him where you're supposed to be. Who should go with you, and who should you leave behind? Be persistent in your prayers and seeking. Be patient with both God and yourself. This is the start of your journey.

Just know this: it will not be easy. No one really talks about how following God can make you feel like you're in a battle. It feels like war—not with the world, but with yourself. Saying yes to God should make life simpler, but instead, it reveals everything inside you that has been out of order before the "YES." It's not just about going to church, singing songs, dressing up, or quoting cute devotionals. It's about absolute and relentless discipline. It's about dying to pride. It's about forgiving people who are not sorry for what they did to you. Forgiving without ever getting the apology you want. It's about getting back up, even if you're the only one who saw you fall.

You need to understand that you are not just

starting over for yourself. Knowing your true identity breaks chains that have held your family for generations—chains of poverty, pain, silence, shame, and survival. Say this with me: "IT STOPS RIGHT HERE! IT STOPS WITH ME!" I had to realize that I wasn't just called to believe; I was called to rebuild. Some days, I am exhausted, to be honest. But I keep going because God is with me. I was built for this. This is who I am—my true identity. His promise to us is that we would never have to fight alone. God steps into that fire with you every single time. It doesn't matter the fight. He is there, no matter the enemy, even when the enemy you're fighting is "you." He's there to help you defeat yourself and come out a better version of yourself on the other side.

The process will not be easy, but it will be worth it. The more we push into Him, the more He reveals to us what needs to be pruned. The more willing we are to face those things directly, no matter how ugly they are, the closer we get to revealing our true nature — our authentic selves.

Starting from scratch can best be understood by looking at the process a caterpillar goes through to become its true self. The butterfly undergoes a fascinating process called metamorphosis, transforming from an egg into a larva (caterpillar), then into a pupa (chrysalis), and finally into an adult butterfly. This four-stage process is a complete metamorphosis, meaning each stage is distinct and serves a different purpose.

Here's a breakdown of each stage and how it could be directly related to a new beginning:

1. **Egg:** The butterfly's life cycle begins when the female butterfly lays eggs, often on or near a food source for the future caterpillar. This stage of starting over from scratch symbolizes rebirth and new beginnings. The egg, as the start of the butterfly's life cycle, embodies this symbolism of renewal and the

continuation of life. When I thought about this, I instantly thought of the word "Hope." The newness and freshness of the egg resemble hope for what can be if I continue to seek God's guidance and allow Him to do the work to transform me into who I need to be.

2. **Larva (Caterpillar):** Once the egg hatches, a larva, or caterpillar, emerges. The caterpillar's main job is to eat and grow, shedding its skin (molting) multiple times as it gets too big. This stage of the process is considered the most crucial because it symbolizes life through intense growth and preparation for transformation. Here is where I am doing a deep dive into God's word. I am intentional about the time I spend with Him. I am strategic in my praying and fasting. I spend every free moment in His presence, allowing Him to show me the things I need to lay at His feet. It is said that during this stage, the primary job of the caterpillar is to EAT and

GROW. So, I feed myself the word of God non-stop. I spend my days listening to sermons that speak to topics relevant to where I am at the moment. I journal my thoughts and prayers. I also journal God's responses to those prayers. You will not emerge in your true identity without consuming the things of God and allowing them to support your continuous growth.

3. **Pupa (Chrysalis):** When the caterpillar reaches its full size, it enters the pupa stage and then forms a chrysalis or cocoon. Inside the cocoon, the caterpillar undergoes a dramatic transformation, breaking down its body and reforming into an adult butterfly. Although it seems dormant, the pupa experiences significant internal changes. This stage represents the potential for new life and marks the end of growth from a crawling larva to a flying insect. For me, this was the hardest part. This is the part where I had

to stay still. It was the part where, on the surface, it looked like nothing was happening. No movements. The calls stopped. The potential mates disappeared. The anxiety of the unknown took over, and the silence once again became the loudest thing in the room. I prayed, but God was silent. I fasted and still saw no movement. What is happening? Am I doing it wrong? Am I not praying right? Suddenly, there was movement in my DMs. The potential mates started to notice me again. I began to have this crazy desire for things I had let go of and hadn't thought of doing in years. This is not right, God. This is the opposite of what is supposed to be happening. You knew my battle with some of these things in the past. You know what it took for me to overcome them. I started to panic because these were some of the things and thoughts that had kept me bound for so long in this identity crisis. One day, while getting out of the shower, God whispered so softly, "Go and read Psalm 46:10." This scripture reads, *"Be still, and know that I am God. I will be exalted among the nations, I will be exalted in the earth!"* This scripture gave me instant confidence that God was at work, and I only needed to be still and wait for the transformation. It caused my anxiety and worry to cease. It allowed me to silently surrender to God's will. I didn't know what or even how; all I knew was that God had it, so it was handled. It allowed me to find peace and assurance in His presence and power over my life. God kept me in that book and had me read that same scripture repeatedly for months. He told me not to stop reading and meditating on it until He said otherwise. When things started to happen that were out of my control, I would throw my hands up, look to heaven, and whisper, "BE STILL, Ira, JUST BE STILL!" This is what I want you to know. Just as He comforted me with His words and His presence, if you let Him, He will do the same for you. I don't care what you think; you won't be able to do this in your own strength. You won't and cannot conquer "You" without God. If you think you can, keep trying. Watch how you just keep running in circles like a hamster on a wheel, going absolutely nowhere. Since you are going to have to bow out eventually, you might as well do it now to save yourself from doing it later. LOL!

4. **Adult Butterfly:** Finally, the adult butterfly emerges from the chrysalis, its wings initially crumpled and wet. The butterfly pumps fluid into its wings, strengthening them for flight, and its main purpose now is to reproduce. Reproduction refers to the biological process by which a new member (or members) of a species is created from a parent (or parents). When the adult butterfly emerges from the

chrysalis, it symbolizes a fresh start, a new beginning. The adult butterfly is a visual representation of change. Isn't that exciting? Not only did it change, but its change was very noticeable. However, that change could also be a bit scary at first, I would imagine. What if the butterfly decided it did not want to change? What if it decided that crawling was easier than flying? Because flying seemed to be more challenging. This is how I used to be. I avoided the hard parts of the journey because they called for me to give up control and let change happen. I was okay crawling. My feet were planted, and I could trust the earth under my feet. Oh, but flying. I have never flown before, and although that is what I was created to do in my true form and identity, I may have to think about it a little longer. The problem with this is that I did not have a little longer. Did you know that if the caterpillar did not go through the changes to become what it was created to become, it is more likely than not that it will die.

My God! That is a lot to take in. Just think about it for a moment. It has no choice but to become what it is predestined to be, or it will die and become nothing at all. Becoming a butterfly was crucial for its survival. Has that sunk in yet? You and I do not have a choice in the matter. We are going to be who God called us to be, or we will simply die without being anything at all.

I feared this change for the same reason the woman in the courtroom with the horrible man did—I didn't want to take the steps. The process might be too long. I want what God wants for me, but honestly, I want it on my terms and in my own timeline. Well, guess what? The butterfly has no control over how long the process from a caterpillar to a butterfly will be. The process can take anywhere from a few weeks to several months. The length of the life cycle depends on the butterfly species. In other words, the creator of the species determines how long the process of the life cycle of His creation will be.

Here's another fact: the caterpillar doesn't consciously choose not to turn into a butterfly. Its metamorphosis is a biological process driven by internal and hormonal factors. That means, it already has everything inside it to do what it needs to do to become what it is supposed to become.

Remember when I told you that God told me the person He made to give me what I needed to push myself and become the best version of myself was me? Yep! He embedded it into my hormones and DNA to just become. I am committed to doing just that. I am committed to simply BECOME.

CHAPTER SIX

IT'S PAINFUL, BUT IT'S NECESSARY

Throughout this journey of growth and becoming my true self, I understand that the pain of growth doesn't feel good while it's happening, but it is essential. Just because it hurts doesn't mean I am doing it wrong. Healing is not a straight path. Sometimes it twists and turns in ways I can't imagine. It brings both great highs and lows.

While healing, allow yourself to feel fully. Don't mask, rush, or suppress your emotions. Just experience all the feelings. Don't numb them with distraction. Sit with them. Cry if you need to. Mourn the old you— the version of yourself and the life you thought you would have when you were pretending to be someone else.

But when you rise, do so with new boundaries and firm limitations. Rise with wisdom and self-respect. Letting go isn't about them, but about finally choosing yourself. Sometimes starting fresh feels like punishment. But remember, God isn't punishing you; He's pruning you—cutting away weeds and dead things. These are what kept you wearing a false identity. They're not welcome in the next chapters of your life. They can't prevent you from reaping God's promises. You are no longer a caterpillar. Crawling is over. Butterflies are meant to fly. So, do it—FLY.

I just know that one day I will look back and thank God for the prayers He did not answer and the doors He did not allow to open. I believe He took away those things I saw as a loss to show me who I was without them. While you are thinking about what I just said, ask yourself: "Were the things I lost worth what they cost me?" Now, tell me you are not grateful God snatched you out and placed you on purpose.

Whenever I start missing the old times, I remind myself that it is not the people or things I miss; it's the version of myself that still believes in that broken kind of love and false connections I was comfortable with. You and I are strong enough to keep moving forward. This pain won't last forever, and you can be sure that the lessons we have learned from it definitely will.

So here we go, it is time. It is time to let it all go. That is where we truly start our healing journey. This is where we begin anew. This is where we seek God for the blueprint to become who we were always meant to be. Here is where we get the courage to stop crawling and prepare our wings for flight.

The only way to find success in this is by giving God FULL access to you. God can only heal what we completely allow Him to. He is an all-or-nothing God. He doesn't do anything halfway. Every time we welcome something God has said "no" to, we tell both Him and our souls that we are not worthy of better.

There is no way a God who said He created us in His image and likeness would be okay with us settling for anything less than the best version of everything we encounter. You must be willing to fully let go of anything that resembles the old version of yourself. This will be difficult because some of these things may hold a special place in your heart. But if they contributed to your identity crisis, they might have to go. Not later, but now. Sometimes you have to rip off the bandage and keep moving forward. I also suggest asking God what needs to go and what can be kept.

For me, I had to do a complete reset. I moved and changed my phone number. I blocked anyone who needed to be blocked on all platforms I used to communicate with them. I unfollowed and deleted numbers. I went through my phone and deleted 10 years' worth of photos and memories. Whenever they pop up—like through a Facebook memory—I would quickly delete them before anything started to linger inside me and remind me of my identity crisis era.

Getting rid of my wedding photos was the hardest

part, but because of the trauma behind the situation, I had to let them go. As much as I wanted to keep them, they were constant reminders of what broke me. I can't heal like that. It took several weeks, but I finally deleted all but one. That one was of me alone. I was beautiful, confident, and felt good about myself. So I kept that one because of the feelings it gave me about myself.

As I close this chapter, I smile because I know something wonderful will come from all this past pain. I want to share what God told me about my new journey while I was spending time with Him. He said that even though the people around me mishandled it, love is never wasted. The love I gave reflected Him because He is love. He also told me how He watched me do what was right even when they did not deserve it.

He loved me, comforted me, and told me never to look at a man again, trying to figure out if I was enough. He said I am enough for Him to die for, which makes me more than enough. He is writing a greater story for me. Just because people abandoned me doesn't mean He ever will. He told me to start seeing myself through His eyes, not through my wounds. They do not define me. He does. Lay down that pain. Cast all your cares on Him. Although your heart is broken, it will not stay that way for long. Victory is ahead, so keep going. Don't look back; there is nothing for you back there. Losing him was not a loss for you, not when I created you to live in abundance.

Now, here is what I want to leave you with. God said that if we allow Him to love us first, He will teach us how to love ourselves, so there will no longer be a need for compromise. Let us embrace His love and presence, and in that embrace, He will give us a strategy for healing and overcoming the cause of our identity crisis. I don't know about you, but I could use a revamp, a do-over, a new start. Although it is scary, I know it will definitely be worth it. So, get up and get going—we have work to do.

The first thing we must do is acknowledge the pain without judging it. I needed to know that my emotions are real and valid. I do not have to be strong every second, and neither do you. Sometimes, days when I am being strong are also the moments when I am falling apart, and I allow God's grace to meet me right where I am. I just tell myself: *Ira, it is okay not to be okay right now. Your feelings are worthy of attention and care.*

The next step is to talk to someone safe. I realized I have a community and do not need to carry this alone. Confide in a friend, therapist, spiritual mentor, or support group. True healing happens through solid connections. When it feels too heavy to say aloud, I write it down in my prayer journal. This helps me vent without having to speak it out loud.

I had to anchor myself spiritually. No matter how rejected I feel at times, I know that God will never abandon me. So, I say to you, tap in. This may be the season you find Him more personally than ever before. His word says in Psalm 34:18 that He is near to the brokenhearted. Just begin each day with a simple prayer. Read scriptures that remind you of your identity and hope.

One of my most effective healing tactics so far has been simply writing my way through it. I started a healing journal. Every day, I write down at least one thing I am thankful for, even if it is just breathing at the moment. I also note how I am feeling right now and how that feeling could positively or negatively affect my day. Additionally, I jot down one truth about myself: "Ira, you are worthy of love, and you are enough just as you are."

Reclaim your body and joy. Trauma often resides in the body. Movement, breathwork, dancing, walking in nature, and singing help release what words cannot. Just a few minutes of these activities daily can begin to reset our nervous system.

Don't forget: you are still whole. This chapter hurts, but it does not define you. You are still yourself — creative, loving, powerful, capable. Healing is not about becoming someone new. It's about returning to who you were before life broke your heart. Take a moment and affirm: "I am not broken — I am breaking through."

Create your own gentle healing routine. I do my best each morning to pray or journal for 10 minutes. It often turns into more, but start where you feel comfortable. At some point during your midday, take a mindful breath break. This involves consciously observing your breath without trying to change it, helping you return to the present moment and manage stress. Before ending your day, reflect on one thing that made you feel supported, peaceful, or seen.

You're not alone in the season of healing. When horrible things happen, or someone walks out — especially a spouse — it can feel like everything good has come crashing down. It can seem like the pages of your life have suddenly gone blank, or worse, been torn out. But here is a beautiful truth: this pain is only a small part of your story, not the whole story. And it certainly is not the end.

Let this chapter, as painful as it may be, become part of your testimony that helps set others free. What is being endured now can be a page someone else reads during their dark day. I am discovering that what felt like an ending is actually an invitation — a divine pause, a moment to be redirected, realigned, and reborn. I am not stuck in the ashes, and neither are you. We are truly being given a chance to rise from them.

Sometimes things fall apart so we can remember that we were never meant to build on them in the first place. So just know this is not the end, only a turning point. God isn't finished yet. God never ends a story on a note of defeat. He's the author who specializes in resurrection, redemption, and restoration. The very thing that was meant to break me became the very thing He is using to build a stronger, better version of me.

Although there are still tough days on this healing journey, I am determined not to give up the mission. The pen remains in my hand, not in the hands of those who broke me. I get to decide what happens next—for how I rise, who I become, and how Ira chooses to love Ira from this day forward. If I keep this in mind, there is something beautiful waiting on the other side of all this pain. I am no longer afraid to try my new wings. If I fall, I will get up and flap them again because, eventually, they will work. I will take flight. I will fly. Honestly, that is what I was meant to do from the very beginning.

Here is a prayer I prayed that might
help you on this healing journey.

God, please help me to stop replaying what hurt me over and over in my mind and to start trusting what lies ahead. Please disconnect all the desires I had for those who only fed and contributed to my wounds. Teach both my heart and my soul to crave peace, not familiar patterns. Sever every soul tie to anything that was never mine in the spirit. Sever what still tugs at my heart and commands its attention.

I declare that every door I would have desired to walk through in my broken state and out of loneliness closes and never opens again. I decree that I will never choose to settle just to feel chosen or to fit in. I release all false identities I adopted to maintain unfruitful relationships. Restore me to my original purpose and identity—who you created me to be before I compromised and lost myself in the pursuit of love. Purify my mind from thoughts and memories that replay because they no longer belong to me. I have cast them at your feet. Release every thought that keeps me trapped in the past version of myself that I have now outgrown.

While I continue to seek you for strategy and guidance, give me the wisdom to prepare for the love you have designed for me. Let it seek me out....a love that feels safe, soft, gentle, and genuine. A solid love. An uncompromising love. The kind that I won't have to chase, question, heal from, or survive. While you are doing that, grow me into the kind of woman (person) who doesn't settle, even when it's lonely, or slow, or at a standstill. Root me so I feel no need to rush into anything or with anybody, for your word says in Jeremiah 29:11 that you know the plans that you have for me, plans to prosper me and not harm me, plans to give me hope and a future. God, I thank you for restoration and a peace that surpasses all understanding.

In Jesus' name, Amen